SCIENTIFIC AMERICAN | EDUCATIONAL PUBLISHING

SCIENTIFIC AMERICAN INVESTIGATES CAREERS IN SCIENCE

COMPUTER SCIENTIST

BY MEGAN QUICK

Published in 2026 by The Rosen Publishing Group
in association with Scientific American Educational Publishing
2544 Clinton Street, Buffalo NY 14224

Library of Congress Cataloging-in-Publication Data
Names: Quick, Megan author
Title: Computer scientist / Megan Quick.
Description: Buffalo, New York : Scientific American Educational Publishing, an imprint of Rosen Publishing, [2026] | Series: Scientific American investigate careers in science | Includes bibliographical references and index. | Audience term: juvenile | Audience: Grades 4-6 Scientific American Educational Publishing, an imprint of Rosen Publishing
Identifiers: LCCN 2025000282 (print) | LCCN 2025000283 (ebook) | ISBN 9781725352537 (library binding) | ISBN 9781725352520 (paperback) | ISBN 9781725352544 (ebook)
Subjects: LCSH: Computer scientists–Juvenile literature | Computer science–Vocational guidance–Juvenile literature | Computer programming–Juvenile literature
Classification: LCC QA76.23 .Q53 2026 (print) | LCC QA76.23 (ebook) | DDC 004–dc23/eng/20250211
LC record available at https://lccn.loc.gov/2025000282
LC ebook record available at https://lccn.loc.gov/2025000283

Designer: Leslie Taylor
Editor: Megan Quick

Portions of this work were originally authored by Jonathan E. Bard and published as *Be an Computer Scientist*. All new material in this edition is authored by Megan Quick.

Photo credits: Cover (main) BongkarnGraphic/Shutterstock.com; series art (background) jijomathaidesigners/Shutterstock.com; p. 5 Halfpoint/Shutterstock.com; p. 7 puhhha/Shutterstock.com, (inset) pisanstock/Shutterstock.com; p. 8 ArtemisDiana/Shutterstock.com; p. 9 monkeybusinessimages/iStockphoto.com; p. 11 fizkes/Shutterstock.com, (inset) Science Museum Group/File:Ada Lovelace portrait.jpg_commons.wikimedia.org; p. 12 Chiffre01/File:Postgres Query.jpg_commons.wikimedia.org p. 13 Gorodenkoff/Shutterstock.com; p. 15 (upper) Alex Photo Stock/Shutterstock.com, (lower) rawf8/Shuttertstock.com; p. 17 Alina555/iStockphoto.com; p. 19 Ohmega1982/Shutterstock.com; p. 21 VectorMine/Shutterstock.com; p. 22 Patricia C. Adams/Shutterstock.com; p. 23 gorodenkoff/iStockphoto.com; p. 25 Miljan Zivkovic/Shutterstock.com; p. 27 Xinhua/Alamy.com; p. 29 insta_photosv/iStockphoto.com.

Printed in the United States of America

CPSIA compliance information: Batch #CSSA26. For Further Information contact Rosen Publishing at 1-800-237-9932.

Find us on

CONTENTS

Words in the glossary appear in **bold** type the first time they are used in the text.

A GROWING FIELD

You probably work with computers at school, and you may have a tablet, phone, or desktop computer at home. You might look up information, do your homework, play games, or chat with friends on a computer. It's a part of your daily life. But do you think about who **designs** websites, who builds the parts that make up your computer, or who came up with the idea for your favorite video game?

It takes many people to design and build computers, and there's always new **technology** coming along. This creates lots of jobs. It's a good time to be thinking about a career in computer science!

Computers are everywhere! Computers in our homes can change the temperature, turn on lights, and set alarms.

GETTING STARTED

If you'd like to work with computers one day, you don't have to wait until you're older. You can start now by learning how to write code. Code is the set of instructions computers need to do everything. Every task a computer completes uses a different code. For example, one code tells your computer to run your favorite program, and a different code lets you send messages to your friends.

Learning how to code can be easy! Some coding languages are ideal for kids, such as Scratch and Python. These programs are easy to follow, so you'll be writing your own code in no time.

FUN FACT

THERE ARE HUNDREDS OF CODING LANGUAGES USED AROUND THE WORLD. IN 2023, SOME OF THE MOST POPULAR PROGRAMMING LANGUAGES WERE JAVASCRIPT, PYTHON, TYPESCRIPT, JAVA, AND C#.

Each coding language has its own rules and style, just like the English language does.

Hello World!

One of the easiest programs to learn is called "Hello, World!" This is simply a program that tells the computer to say hello in a message box. Programmers begin with this program because it gives a clear result. They know they've correctly programmed when they see the message box.

MANY CHOICES

There are many areas of computer science. Once you get to college, you will choose an area that you would like to **specialize** in. You will start by taking general classes. From there, you will see what interests you.

If you like biology or medicine, you might choose to focus on a field like **bioinformatics**. If you want to keep **data** safe, you can take classes to become a security analyst. You might decide you want to design and program websites. One great thing about computer science is that the choices are nearly endless, since computers have so many uses.

Some students spend time as computer science interns in college. An intern is someone who works for a company to learn and gain real-life experience.

Computers Fighting Disease

Programmers can use computers to help fight deadly diseases. Bioinformaticians write programs that look at huge amounts of medical data. They use math to find patterns in the data. For disease **research**, bioinformaticians work closely with doctors and other scientists. They learn how diseases start, and they figure out ways to help sick people.

CODES AND BUGS

Computers may seem smart, but they need smart people to tell them what to do. Computer programmers tell computers what to do by using coding languages. Programmers need to know many different languages to tackle all kinds of projects.

Programmers often work with a partner. They discuss what a program needs to do, how the code should be written, and how the program will be made. Then they write the code. They check each other's code to find and fix any bugs, or errors in the program. Working with a partner cuts down on the number of bugs, and it makes the final program better.

FUN FACT

MANY PEOPLE CONSIDER ADA LOVELACE TO BE THE FIRST COMPUTER PROGRAMMER. IN THE MID-1800S, COMPUTERS WERE SIMPLE MACHINES USED TO **CALCULATE** NUMBERS. ADA FOUND THAT MACHINES COULD DO MORE THAN MATH: THEY COULD FOLLOW INSTRUCTIONS.

Ada Lovelace

Programming often starts with trading ideas with team members.

DEALING WITH DATA

Pictures, videos, music, numbers, and words are examples of computer data. All this information is stored and organized in databases, so when people need a piece of data, they can find it quickly. In this way, databases are a lot like libraries!

Computer scientists who create and use databases are called database administrators. They often work for large businesses that have a lot of data to store. Database administrators write programs to organize the information so others can easily **access** the data. They also make sure the data is secure, or safe, and won't be lost if there is a problem with the computer system.

Business databases contain huge amounts of data that is organized so that it's easy to find.

SMART SYSTEMS

Computer scientists who help computers stay up and running are called system administrators. They know a great deal about the operating systems they manage. An operating system is the main program that starts up when the computer is powered on. It controls everything the computer does.

System administrators identify and fix problems with computer systems. When a system needs to be updated, they find and test new **software** and hardware to make sure that it works well for their organization.

System administrators work with people as well as computers. They answer questions and help with any problems workers might have with their computer system.

The two most popular operating systems today are MacOS and Windows.

SAFE AND SECURE

Your computer knows a lot about you! The more we use computers, the more information we give them. Everything from birthdates to banking records may be online. The people who protect this information are called security analysts.

People who use their computer skills to steal information are known as hackers. Hackers write programs called **viruses**, and they can be sent out through emails or files. Users may then run these programs by accident. When they do, these viruses can take users' information and send it back to the hackers. Security analysts write programs that search users' computers to find viruses planted by hackers.

FUN FACT

CYBERCRIME, OR A CRIME THAT HAPPENS WITH A COMPUTER, COULD COST THE WORLD OVER $15 TRILLION BY 2029. THIS AMOUNT INCLUDES STOLEN MONEY, DESTROYED DATA, AND THE COST OF FIXING HACKED SYSTEMS.

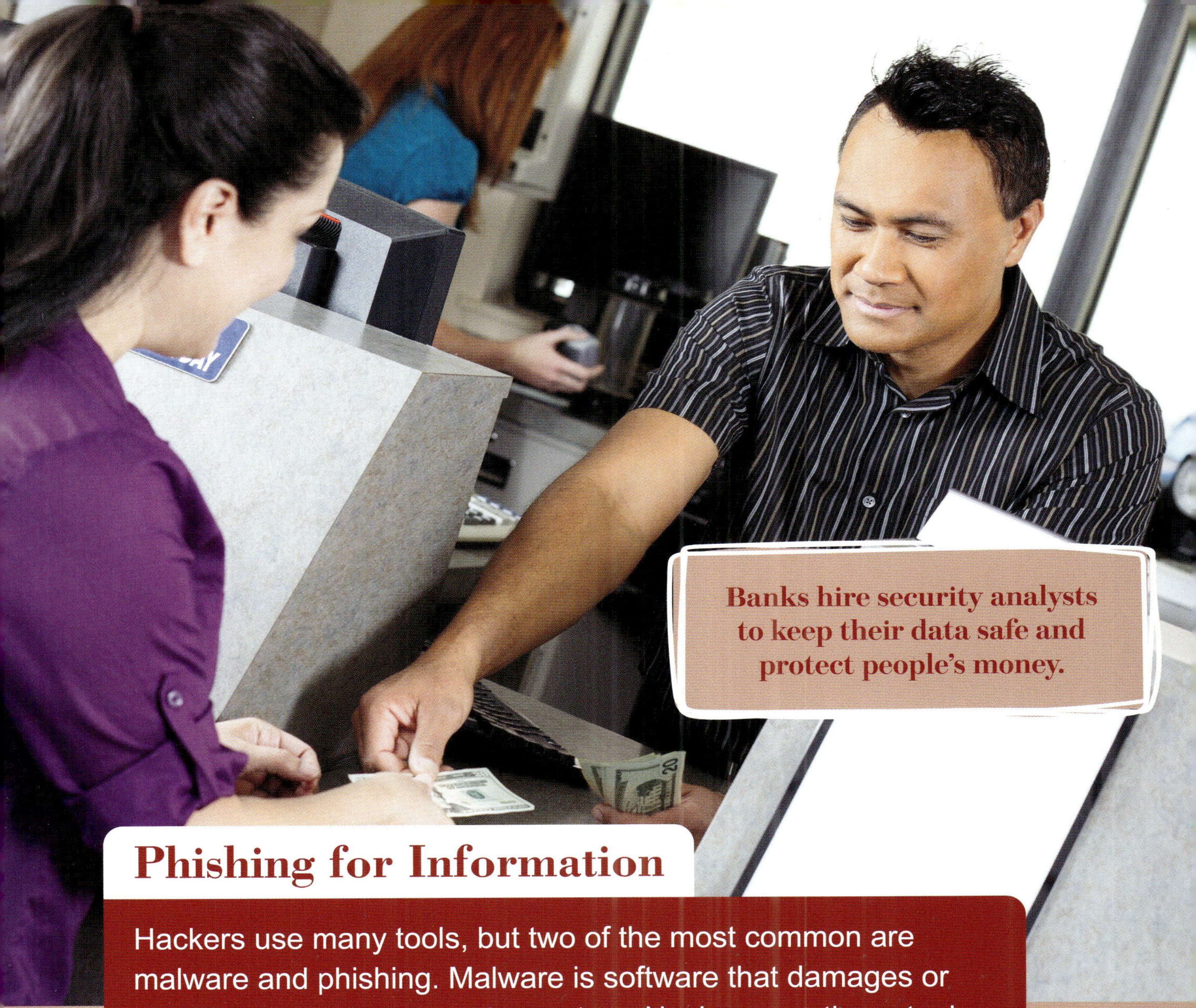

Banks hire security analysts to keep their data safe and protect people's money.

Phishing for Information

Hackers use many tools, but two of the most common are malware and phishing. Malware is software that damages or provides entry to a computer system. Hackers can then steal data or even take over the computer. Phishing occurs when hackers send emails or texts that trick a user into giving out information like passwords or credit card information.

CONNECTING COMPUTERS

Places like schools and offices use many computers. These computers need to be connected to each other so people can share information. These connected computers are called a computer network. Network engineers make sure a network is fast and stable so that the people using it can get their work done without issues.

If lots of devices are connected to the network at the same time, the network needs to be able to handle all that traffic. Network engineers design and set up networks to handle the demands of their users. Like a security analyst, a network engineer also makes sure that the network is safe from hackers.

Computer Network

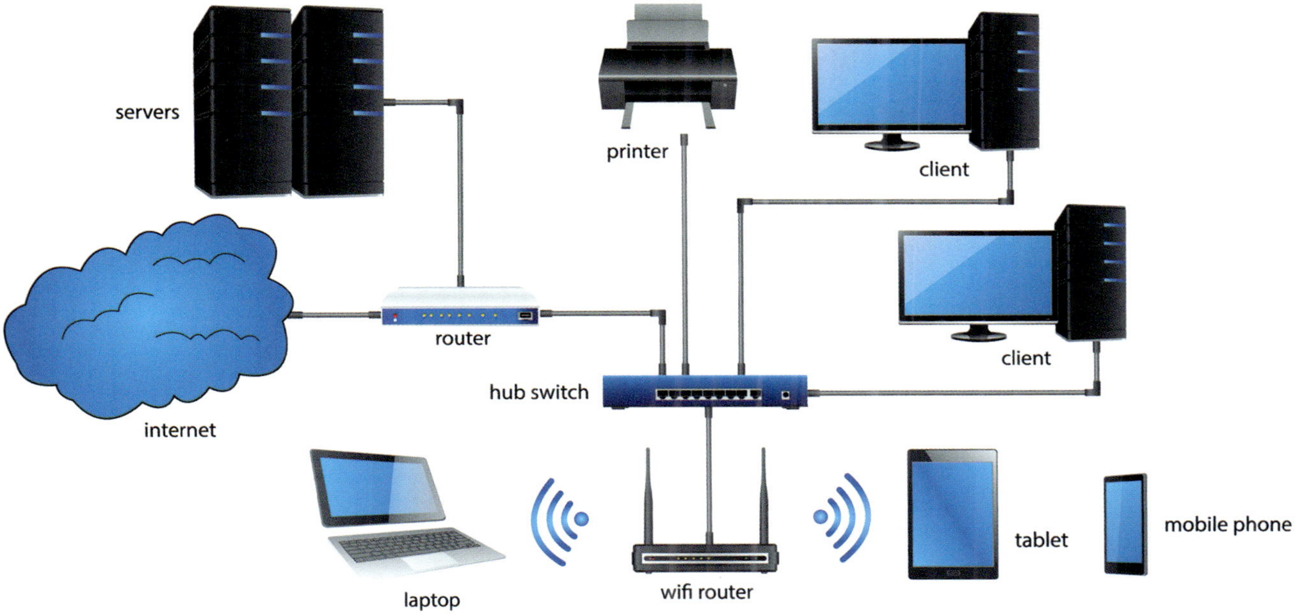

In a computer network, the switch connects the computers, the router allows the computers to share an internet connection, and the server stores and shares data that's used by the network.

Internet vs. World Wide Web

Do you know the difference between the internet and the World Wide Web? The internet is a huge network of connected computers around the world. The web is all the pages that you find on the internet. You cannot access the web without first connecting to the internet.

PUTTING THE PARTS TOGETHER

The **physical** parts of a computer are called hardware. Hardware engineers design, build, and test these parts. They are always looking for ways to make computers work better.

Hardware engineers make sure all parts of a computer work well together. If they don't, it could be because some parts are older than others, or they might be made for one type of computer and not useable in others.

Hardware engineers may specialize in one area. They may be test engineers who focus on making sure a part works properly. They might also be design engineers who create prototypes, or early models, of a part during the design stage.

Computer Hardware

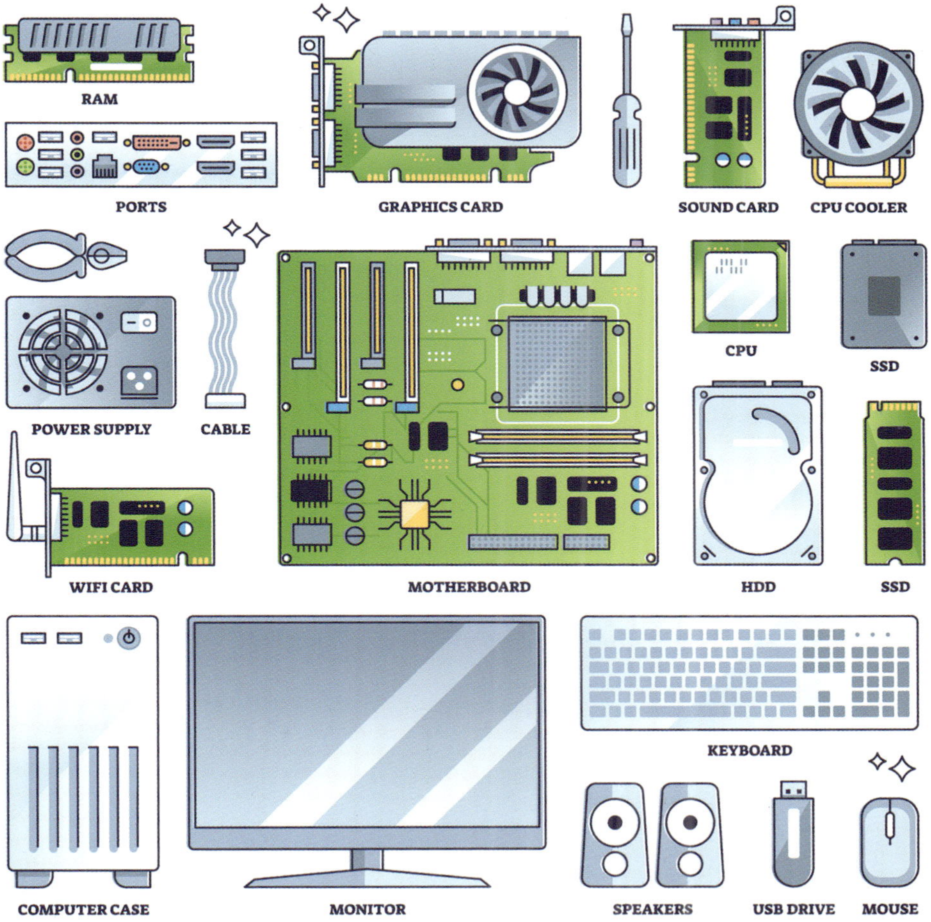

Hardware engineers design, build, and maintain the computer parts shown here. The motherboard, at center, connects the many electronic parts to each other.

WORKING ON THE WEB

If you want to watch videos, get homework help, or chat with friends, you can head to your favorite website in just a few clicks. There are websites for just about any purpose you can think of. But who designs them? Web developers create all parts of the websites we visit every day.

Web developers build websites for big companies, small organizations, and everything in between. They first have to think about how people will **interact** with the website. Then, they write code that both makes the website enjoyable for users to visit and encourages users to share it with family and friends.

FUN FACT

IN 2024, THE MOST WIDELY VISITED WEBSITE IN THE WORLD WAS GOOGLE. IN SECOND AND THIRD PLACE WERE YOUTUBE AND FACEBOOK.

facebook YouTube Google

A web developer makes sure that people using websites such as online stores can easily find (and buy) what they need.

FUN AND GAMES

Chances are that you've spent time, alone or with friends, playing video games. They can be really fun, but they're also a lot of work to make! First, game designers come up with the ideas for the game itself. Game developers then take those ideas and figure out details such as what the game will look like and how the users will interact with the game.

A video game project takes many people with different skills all working as a team. Programmers write the code for the game, while system administrators keep the game servers running. Network engineers make sure players can connect from all around the world.

If you're serious about video games, you can go to a college that offers courses in video game development and design.

THE RISE OF AI

One of the newest fields in computer science is Artificial Intelligence (AI). With AI, computers are able to perform tasks that could once only be done by humans. This includes learning, creating, making decisions, and solving problems. AI engineers design and develop programs for a wide range of uses, from robots and self-driving cars to healthcare and farming.

AI engineers teach computers to "think" based on experience. They do this by feeding computers large amounts of data. Over time, the computer responds based on patterns it sees in the data. The computer can learn to identify objects, understand language, and even act on its own.

FUN FACT

THE FIRST AI PROGRAM WAS WRITTEN IN 1951. A COMPUTER SCIENTIST NAMED CHRISTOPHER STRACHEY "TAUGHT" A COMPUTER TO PLAY AN ENTIRE GAME OF CHECKERS.

In 2024, AI helped these robots kick, shoot, and dribble a ball during a soccer game.

AI In Space

The use of AI has quickly spread to all areas of science and technology, all the way to space. Machines called rovers have safely explored Mars and sent data back to Earth with the help of AI. It also allows spacecraft to fly without humans on board so that scientists can test new technology without endangering people.

YOUR FUTURE CAREER?

If you're interested in becoming a computer scientist, it's never too early to start preparing. Check out coding programs, whether they are classes, camps, or online. In high school, take classes in computer science as well as math. As a computer science major in college, you'll take classes that will help you decide which areas interest you the most.

Computer science is an exciting area that is always changing and growing. More and more, computers play a huge role in business as well as our everyday lives. As a computer scientist, you can play a part in creating new technology while helping people stay connected.

Computer classes and camps are everywhere. These students are learning about coding and computers while building robotic cars.

GLOSSARY

access: To be able to use, enter, or get near.

bioinformatics: The collection, classifying, and storage of biological information using computers.

calculate: To find by performing mathematical operations (such as addition, subtraction, multiplication, and division).

data: Information created and stored by a computer.

design: To plan and develop ideas for how a program or piece of hardware will work, and then carrying out the plan.

interact: To act upon one another.

physical: Having material existence.

research: The collecting of information about a subject.

server: The central computer that supplies data for the other computers to use.

software: The programs and related information used by a computer.

specialize: To become very good at one particular thing.

technology: Using science, engineering, and other industries to invent useful tools or to solve problems. Also a machine, piece of equipment, or method created by technology.

virus: A computer program that harms a computer.